WHO BROKE MY DAUGHTER'S ALABASTER BOX?

BY

C.M. JAMES

Who Broke My Daughter's Alabaster Box?

C. M. James

Midwest Creations Publishing

St. Louis, MO 63114

Visit our website at https://midwest-creations-publishing.square.site

Who Broke My Daughter's Alabaster Box?

ISBN:

…this book is dedicated to my friend, one of my editors, a woman after God's own heart: <u>Teresa Taylor Williams</u>, you are a true gift of God to all. Love you, girl.

Table of Contents

Luke 19:45-47

45 *Then He went into the temple [enclosure] and began to drive out those who were selling,*

46 *Telling them, It is written, My house shall be a house of prayer; but you have made it a [b]cave of robbers.*

47 *And He continued to teach day after day in the temple [porches and courts]. The chief priests and scribes and the leading men of the people were seeking to put Him to death...* (AMPC – Amplified Classic)

SECTION I: MY BEAUTIFUL SISTERS

Lesson One: RENE

Rene Barnes was no fool. Well, yeah, she'd made her mistakes as a kid in high school. Though she didn't consider Jabari, her twelve-year-old son, a mistake.

She had been young, impressionable and wet behind the ears, like most sixteen-year olds.

And like most young girls fresh in the chat rooms when the internet-at-home phase had just begun, she had been gullible to the hard, ugly truths of this world.

Rene had bought Jabari's father's lies like she'd had a free shopping spree at the mall. Eager to be loved, with the blah-blah-blah daddy issues her counselor touted had controlled her actions; Rene experienced her first love.

With a teacher's aide ten years older and a whole lot wiser. Or so she thought.

Bookworms didn't usually garner the attention of attractive men. To say she'd been out of her element would be putting it mildly.

And with pressure coming from her mom about getting a high score on her upcoming ACT tests, along with homecoming dances (that she didn't have a date to) and her first prom coming up (which she wouldn't have a date to), Rene had been vulnerable to the wise, older guy routine.

That had been a long time ago. Suffice it to say, her start at Lindenwood University in St. Charles, Missouri had been delayed, but not destroyed.

A campus well equipped to handle small families, Rene, too strong-minded to quit (especially with Jabari depending on her), was determined to finish and finish well.

And she did. Graduating cum-laude with a career waiting on her in the data sciences and infrastructure field, Rene took life by storm in a way that Jabari would never want for anything, whether his father decided to chip in to help or not. Which he didn't. Ever.

Rene was totally okay with Jabari's father being an absentee dad. They were doing just fine. She had her family, her son and her Jesus. Rene was content. Most of the time.

Most of the time was a stretch. Because Rene had a problem. A man problem. A lust problem. A, why do I have to be the one that grew up in church and was taught that a woman's body is sacred and not to be defiled by every Tom, Harry and Joe kind of problem.

The hard truth was, despite Rene having everything she needed, she couldn't help but notice the empty space in her life.

Her friends on Facebook and Instagram were constantly posting pictures of their anniversaries, their outings, their lovey-doviness.

Why didn't she qualify for that? It's not like she hadn't put herself out there. She had. And it had been a horrible experience.

The dating apps, even the Christian ones were a joke. People masked wanting to find a life partner for wanting a quick hook up. There were men who just needed a place to stay crowding her message boxes. She couldn't post a picture on Instagram without someone being all, "hey beautiful, saw your picture, you're beautiful."

Rene had grown so tired of all that. Her mom, Janice Roth, had given her the low down on finding "the one."

"There ain't no ONE baby, there is the best that you are going to get. No one is perfect. You're not, men are not. Your best bet is to let a Godly man that loves God with all his heart, mind and being find YOU. Trust me, everything else out there sets you up to fail. A man that can't submit to God, don't need a wife or kids. That's the truth."

Taking her mother's words to heart, Rene had done what a sensible, Christian raised woman would do.

She'd gone back to church. Well, joined the local church that was two blocks away anyway.

The Pastor seemed nice, the people welcomed her and Jabari with open arms and she was totally in agreement with their statement of faith.

Enter Minister Darnell Peterson. Married, Minister Darnell Peterson. Whose wife never came to church because she'd backslid into drugs and who knows what else according to Darnell.

Rene and Darnell both shared a teaching gift and worked within the youth ministry. They had so much in common. Both of them worked downtown so it was easy to run into each other on lunch breaks. Lunch breaks that became youth ministry meetings. Meetings that became a lunch date where phone numbers had been exchanged. The numbers exchanged became late night rap sessions that revealed just how much they had in common… and how much they wanted to be with each other.

Rene knew that she was smart. She wasn't a silly woman by any means. But her heart knew what it wanted.

Darnell had just married the wrong woman, she reasoned. He had messed up with her and, maybe, God was giving him another chance. With Rene.

While she didn't know much about his wife except for what he'd told her, she did know that everyone in the church seemed to feel sad for him a lot. Rene could only imagine what the woman put him through.

Darnell began to come for visits; throw around the football with Jabari and come to his games. Jabari loved the man. And so did Rene.

It was clear to her what God was telling her. Darnell would be her husband. That said, since it had been six months and they'd gotten to the point of heavy make out sessions; Rene decided it was time to have "the talk" with Darnell,.

Determined to approach him with their need to plan the future after youth service that day, Rene tripped over her own feet when she seated Jabari and turned to place her bible in the pew.

Darnell stood at the door with the Pastors cuddled around a young woman. A sick young woman. A sick young woman with a wedding ring. His gaze toward her had been imploring, filled with silent pleas as the frail thing clung to him for support.

Rene's lips thinned. Her hands balled tightly into fists. Jabari, knowing the signs of his mother's anger apparently, followed her gaze to what stood at the door.

He snapped back in his seat and jerked his head back toward the front of the church. Rene knew a lot about her son. And one thing she knew, is that he wasn't stupid either.

As the group slowly made their way up the aisle, Rene dropped into her seat beside Jabari and gripped the edge of the pew. The shock was slowly giving way to anger. And fear.

Darnell's hand landed softly on her's as the group passed her by.

Snatching her hand away while appearing nonchalant was the hardest thing Rene had ever had to do.

She loved him. Rene seriously loved this man. She'd given him six months of her life. And access to her son. Surely there had to be a good explanation for this?

Looking to the raised platform where the Pastor stood with meager hope, she waited for some message of enlightenment; some explanation that would clarify what was happening, that would verify that Darnell had not been lying to her all this time.

Only, it was a disappointing truth that came across the pulpit instead. Darnell, nephew by marriage to the Pastor and his wife (by the way) was ecstatic at the testimony he and his wife had received from her doctors. Stage three cancer was a terminal thing. Chemotherapy and radiation are what had caused her emaciation. But praise God, she was coming back with a remission report, according to the Pastor.

God was healing his niece! Darnell's wife. Rene's future husband Darnell. He'd lied to her. He'd lied to Jabari with his actions. How could she have been so stupid and so blind?

***

I wanted to start this off with Rene's story because I know that many of us can sympathize; at least a little bit.

Back in November 2010, statistics showed that seventy percent of black children were born into single parent families. Now, keep in mind, this is only counting those that are not legally married couples, other statuses such as couples living together or couples that considered themselves "together", are not counted as such.

Also, the rate of single fathers today is growing rapidly, thus we cannot assume that this number includes ALL mothers. However, the number is still staggering.

In 2019 the rate of single white, non-hispanic women that are new mothers hovered around 6,695. The total (please remember that Caucasians are the majority in the United States) 6.69 million single mothers.

There are 4.15 million Black families with a single mother, an increase of 1.11 million since 1990.

In 2015 the gender gap of men to women was at four percent. That doesn't seem like much, but we are talking MILLIONS. Further, sixty percent of the male population was aged sixty or above.

I'm providing these numbers so that we can see the truth surrounding the "big picture" here.

I heard a statistic once that a woman is more likely to get hit by a car than to marry after age forty.

And I was horrified. Because I wanted to be married.

While we won't delve into other related statistics such as how many of those men are incarcerated, below legal age, gay/transgender etc, I will expound on this truth:

GOD WILL NEVER GIVE YOU A HUSBAND THAT IS ALREADY MARRIED.

Hard truth time sis.

Most of us are reasonably intelligent. Yet most of us have, at some point or other, been tricked into compromising. I don't have to lay down these facts in writing because you already know them.

If you found your husband by him cheating on a spouse, nine times out of ten, he will do the same with you.

And, I must be real with you regarding Rene. No matter the sob story and situation, no matter how true what is spoken is, the bottom line is that God will NOT tell you that a married man is your husband. Period.

Check out the book of Malachi, chapter 2.

> **10** *Do we not all have one Father? Has not one God created us? Why do we deal treacherously with one another,*

profaning the covenant of our fathers
[with God]? **11** Judah has been
treacherous (disloyal), and an repulsive
act has been committed in Israel and in
Jerusalem; for Judah has profaned the
sanctuary of the LORD which He loves,
and has married the daughter of a
foreign god. **12** As for the man who does
this, may the LORD cut off from the tents
of Jacob to the last man those who do
this [evil thing], awake and aware, even
the one who brings an offering to
the LORD of hosts.

13 This is another thing you do: you
cover the altar of the LORD with tears,
with [your own] weeping and sighing,
because the LORD no longer regards
your offering or accepts it with favor
from your hand. **14** But you say, "Why
[does He reject it]?" Because
the LORD has been a witness between
you and the wife of your youth, against
whom you have dealt treacherously. Yet
she is your marriage companion and
the wife of your covenant [made by

your vows]. **15** *But not one has done so who has a remnant of the Spirit. And what did that one do while seeking a godly offspring? Take heed then to your spirit, and let no one deal treacherously against the wife of your youth.* **16** *"For I hate [a]divorce," says the* LORD*, the God of Israel, "and him who covers his garment with wrong and violence," says the* LORD *of hosts. "Therefore keep watch on your spirit, so that you do not deal treacherously [with your wife]."* **AMP (Amplified)**

See what I mean? This is God telling you FLAT OUT that another woman's husband is not yours.

I know. I KNOW. I have honestly been in a situation, finding out too late (after conceiving a daughter) that the man I had set my future on was already married, with a mistress no less. By mistress I mean ANOTHER woman besides me. I struggled. I told him that he needed to get a divorce. But I promise you, I was still wrong in being there waiting in the wings while he did. Only, in the end, for God to tell me to leave that situation; that this man was NOT a husband for me.

It didn't matter that we shared a child. He shared 3 with his ex-wife and 2 with his mistress. What mattered was that he was NOT for me, and God made that clear.

I'm writing this to encourage you my sister, as well as call you into accountability.

I do it with a heavy heart and much pain, for this route leads to much pain for you. And, like your Father in Heaven, I would spare you that if I could.

There is no situationship, no relationship, no anything without a proper covenant before God for you. Anything else is beneath you, for you ARE the daughter of the GREAT KING.

The oil in your alabaster box is a rare and precious prize, not to be wasted upon the body or feet of a man that does not walk in the image of Christ.

Do not waste this treasure on a man that disdains God. He can never understand how to treasure you or what you hold dear otherwise.

Your emotions are YOURS. Temptation is rampant. There will be men that will call to you like sirens to a sailor. You have to guard your heart above all things and wave that foolishness away.

To settle for less than the covenant of power that God would gift you in a marital relationship is to create for yourself a prison that you could never free yourself from.

That is not what your Father intends for you.

Lesson Two: The Spirit of The Wolf

The Spirit of the wolf, spirit of division, devouring spirit, whatever name you'd like to call it, comes in many forms.

One particular form is the embodiment of a false teacher, preacher or minister that has one goal in mind, to separate the sheep from the fold in order to devour them.

This lesson focuses on THAT wolf. The wolf that is a Pastor or authority figure among single, vulnerable, women. Women who long for validation, leadership, and safety.

God's house is to be a haven for these women. Typically, within the Kingdom of God (God's way of doing things) women are encouraged to submit to one having authority over them if they have no husband.

The word submit is a controversial term during these days of women's liberation to the point of menemasculation (yes I made that word up; basically it means the cultures attempt to completely emasculate the embodiment of what is considered male or "manly" due to its war against assigned gender roles). We don't have time for this particular argument, so let's focus on the lesson at hand.

As you are aware of the staggering statistics from lesson one, the truth remains that there will be more single women than available men currently (except for in Alaska where there are 108 men for every 100 women).

Let's talk about submission, which is NOT blind obedience, by the way.

The Latin root of submit means to "bend to", to make allowance for, to subtly and seriously consider the one that you are submitting to, as a source of provision and security.

I like to put it this way. Women are Man version 2.0. And just like smartphones – as they got smarter, they became more vulnerable, woman is the more vulnerable part of mankind. I'm not saying she's better because she's version 2.0. I'm saying there are processes that she is built with, including the ability to make a person similar to herself and the seed bearer, that man version 1.0 doesn't have. She processes on the spot via communication, whereas Man must process in a more linear fashion; not as he communicates, but before he communicates. If he attempts otherwise, it can lead to what they call "foot-in-the-mouth" disease.

Warning, my sister. I know it sounds like you can argue a man into a corner just because you process as you communicate. But trust me, if a man goes silent in an argument, it doesn't mean that you've won, it means that he is processing. He may come back two days later with points that will blow your mind on an argument you thought you'd already settled. Just because he takes longer to process due to the linear method, doesn't mean he lacks the ability.

Back on topic, as Man 2.0 (or woman, translated from womb-man), due to your many faceted nature created specifically to support, strengthen and uphold man (word for woman in Greek was "paracletos", similar to the word used for the Holy Spirit; meaning to support, strengthen, uphold... kind of like a support beam with a building), your casing is more vulnerable in order to add a nurturing aspect (breast feeding, etc.) for the offspring you will carry.

In order for security and protection to be upheld in the family unit, there have to be clear cut roles. This prevents chaos and confusion. The least vulnerable of the two, man 1.0 is usually in charge of safety and security. Meaning man 2.0 must be willing to "bend" when needed to ensure the entire family units safety.

God made provision for those without a covering (man 1.0). His house.

The church is the BODY of Christ. Let's be clear about that. Not a building. The BODY.

It is a rare condition for one part of the body to attack and harm another. A body such as that is ill, diseased and is not very efficient.

The Body of Christ has always been intended as a HOUSE for the Spirit of the Lord.

Not only us individually, but the body of Christ corporately.

Hold on, I'm getting there, I promise.

So, here's my point.

All single women have a right to seek safety in the body of Christ. They should never have to fear being vulnerable. They should never have to fear being taken advantage of. They should never have to fear being lied to or falsely accused.

Yet, there are men, women... LEADERS in the body of Christ, who have forgotten that they are responsible for God's people.

The spirit of the wolf has infiltrated God's House.

Beloved's this ought not be so!!!

How have we allowed this false teacher, false prophet, lying spirit, to enter in?

Men and women placed in authority by God have allowed themselves to fall prey to it and have purposely led astray and defiled God's people.

Let me be clear. GOD IS NOT PLEASED.

Judgement always begins at the house of the Lord. I tell you truly my sisters, God's judgment is coming for those that He has placed in authority who have used and abused his people.

He will NOT allow this to continue.

The spirit of the wolf operates similarly to Darnell in the first lesson. Darnell knew that Rene was a new church member, thus unaware of his current marital situation.

Darnell was selfish in his desires to have what his wife could not give him due to illness and sought comfort from another; not caring or even considering how the situation would end for that person.

He callously entrenched himself in Rene's life, making a point to endear himself to her son. Because sis, the truth is the truth: if a way to a man's heart is through his stomach, a way to a woman's heart is through her children.

Darnell purposefully seated himself in a place that he had no right to. It was not his place. It was never his place. He belonged to another; and Rene, until she was claimed by a man of God and under his protection, belonged to God.

What you didn't notice (as it was unspoken) though it was easy to read between the lines, was how Darnell subtly kept Rene from seeking out friendships within the church, by monopolizing a lot of her free time.

Rene could have easily learned the truth had she gone about forming relationships with other church members. But that didn't happen.

Darnell kept her separated or divided from the others.

That is how the spirit of the wolf works, friends.

It comes to divide and, like Satan, its goal is to kill, steal, and destroy.

There are Pastors, Minsters, Evangelists, Teachers, Prophets and Apostles that have taken advantage of God's people; raping and molesting them of resources and dignity, mentally and physically.

And here is what God's word has to say about them.

Malachi 2

Who Broke My Daughter's Alabaster Box?
By C. M. James

"Now, O priests, this commandment is for
you. ² If you do not listen, and if you do not
take it to heart to honor My name," says
the LORD of hosts, "then I will send the curse
upon you and I will curse your blessings [on
the people]. Indeed, I have cursed them
already, because you are not taking it to
heart. ³ Behold, I am going to rebuke your
seed, and I will spread the refuse on your
faces, the refuse from the festival offerings;
and you will be taken away with it [in
disgrace]. ...

⁷ For the lips of the priest should
guard and preserve knowledge [of My law],
and the people should seek instruction from
his mouth; for he is the messenger of
the LORD of hosts. ⁸ But as for you [priests],
you have turned from the way and you
have caused many to stumble by your
instruction [in the law]. You have violated
the covenant of Levi," says the LORD of
hosts. ⁹ "So I have also made you despised
and abased before all the people, just as
you are not keeping My ways but are
showing partiality [to people] in [your
administration of] the law."

To take advantage of God's children is to dishonor God's name and God's nature.

It has never been God's intention for his leaders to misuse and mishandle those precious to Him. He does not like it and He will not stand for it.

Sister, I heartily urge you; if you are attending a church where you know for a fact that this is happening; or you are participating (or complicit in actively promoting such an atmosphere); I urge you to ask forgiveness, repent and exit stage left.

That particular house is already destined to fall. God has set himself against that leadership and any prayer that they pray per what you just read in Malachi.

What did I mean about complicit? Simply this: If men are not your husband, they are your brothers and fathers in the ministry. This is a FAMILY; the body of Christ is. And just as incest is a shameful thing, it is so when a woman or man purposefully seeks sexual gratification within the body of Christ (this does not give us license to do so outside the body, my point is that it is much more of a disgraceful act to do so with a family member than one outside of the family).

Case in point, if the church is filled with your brothers and fathers, your clothing should be circumspect, respectful and protective of your father's and brother's vulnerability when it comes to visual stimuli.

And yes, I am attacking the liberation front once again that states, "I should be able to wear whatever I want to wear; its my body, I should do whatever I want to do with my body".

As Paul says, all things are good, but they are not helpful. You can wear what you want, you have that freedom, okay fine. But is it showing love for your brother who you know, has an inherent biological imperative that forces him, every four seconds, to think of ways to propagate the human race?

So, you would drink in front of an alcoholic? Smoke in the face of a smoker? Or would you be respectful of their struggle?

The point that I am making is that just as your brothers and fathers are supposed to be protecting you, you are supposed to be protecting THEM. If you actively flaunt your sexuality before your brethren then you are COMPLICIT in their action of seeking gratification with you. You must take accountability in this if this is something you do or have done. I will not lie. I have done it.

I am a well-endowed woman. There have been times when I have worn clothing that I knew, were I a wife, I would not like it being flaunted around my husband.

In the past, I have justified this error saying that the onus is upon the man to train himself NOT to look.

Okay, that may be true. But am I showing LOVE to my brother by doing this?

Or does loving him mean UNDERSTANDING his weakness and making sure that I do not contribute to the several temptations he encounters via television commercials, billboards, social media ads and everyday foot traffic that he already has to deal with in any given day?

Here is where we must be accountable my sisters. Tell yourself the truth regarding your own motives; why you do what you do? Is it an act of love, or a desire to receive validation from men that do not belong to you? God does not judge you. He loves you. But He wants you free. If your motives are not pure, freedom will prove elusive for you. You become a slave to your desires and act them out accordingly. God wants better for you. And so do I.

That said, let's be clear about those that are NOT complicit. Those that are vulnerable – you've lost a loved one, you've lost a job, you don't know where your next meal is coming from, you have recently come out of an abusive situation, you are in desperate need of help form a counsellor and are mentally unstable – all of these are examples of the truly vulnerable that should have been protected, not taken advantage of in the body of Christ.

I will repeat this for the cheap seats in the back: The church is to be a safe haven for the women that belong to God such as these.

For them to be touched or abused by those given positions to watch over the flock is an abomination and hateful thing in the eyes of God.

Scripture shows that women are prey to the spirit of the Wolf that hides in the form of man.

Paul plainly states, "for these are the men that go into the houses of silly women and lead them astray."

Women have one vulnerability: MAN. Read Genesis; when God is doling out consequences for the fall of man, his consequence to the woman is, "will greatly multiply your pain in child birth... yet your desire and longing will be for your husband, and he will rule over you." And to the serpent, He promised, "I will create enmity between you and the woman; her offspring will crush your head and you will bruise his heel."

Okay, right there, we see that woman is the enemy of Satan. Period. Why do you think you have an innate ability to sense when things are off? Things that are about to go wrong? Spiritually divisive situations that send chills up your spine? Because your enemy is at work and God gave you a built-in alarm to see him coming.

But your enemy is smart, and he knows your weakness. Man, himself, who you long for and are filled with desire for.

So, what does he do? He sends the man-clothed spirit of the wolf to divide you from all who know and love you, in order to devour you. YOU are his enemy. He comes for you because while man may cover us physically, we are an alarm system that should be covering THEM spiritually.

You said all of that to say what sis?

Only the enemy, Satan himself, was bold enough to walk into God's house and seduce his daughter.

That's what I'm saying. A leader that would do such a thing is a child of the enemy HIMSELF and you need to leave that place in all haste.

There is nothing good there until God ousts the offender and installs new leaders into his house.

You want to sow in good ground. You want your prayers to be heard corporately. Do not remain in a place that has shown such disrespect to the Lord.

Don't listen to people and their arguments; listen to GOD. Go where He sends you sis; I promise you won't be disappointed.

ACTION STEPS:

IF you have found yourself in these situations:

1. **SEEK WISE COUNSEL** – find someone that you know will keep your confidence and partner with you in being accountable for your choices, to pray with you, and to help support you as you transition back into your rightful position or into a spirit filled church home to be planted.

2. **SEEK GOD** – He loves you. He will never leave you nor forsake you. Willingly give to Him all of the issues of your heart. He binds up the broken hearted and heals all their wounds and

sorrows. He knows what you need, and He will be there to help you break the chains, soul ties and other painful attachments that you share with a married man.

3. **CUT TIES** – Let him go. Or let the church itself go in that second circumstance. In every way. Block his number on your phone. Block him on all social media. Make sure his calls are screened at work. Change your pattern of behavior. Make it extremely difficult for him to get to you. Enlist family and friends in this endeavor. He knows the words to say that will convince you to come back. Don't give him that opportunity. Sis, this is going to hurt. If you have ever died to yourself in your life, this will be just that. The pain will feel close to the pain of losing a loved one. But it is nothing compared to the pain of finding yourself a victim of his cheating later in life. Let him go. Or let them go. Give him/them to God.

4. **STAY FOCUSED ON GOD** – pursuing a different relationship would be a mistake (unless we are talking about your finding a spirit-filled church home). Instead, use your

smart phone as a recording journal. Voice record your daily progress. How you feel, what God is saying, scriptures you read, and what your accountability partner has counselled you to do. Play them over again every four weeks. You will hear your voice growing stronger, more confident, less riddled with pain and, instead, filled with the renewal of God's presence. Mark the dates on your calendar that you notice a change. You're smiling more. You're able to go places again without feeling that twinge. Mark every victory as the Lord restores your soul. I promise you won't regret it. You deserve better, and this is the perfect time to focus on you. Focus on you allowing God to show you what BETTER looks like.

5.   **USE YOUR TOOLS** - Last, use the notepad in your phone (or buy a journal) and start writing. Write down what your dreams and desires were before you met him or started going to that church. Write down goals you'd lost sight of along the way and how God is now redirecting your desires back to it. Remember, you're not seeking another relationship right now, you are seeking healing, wholeness, and

restoration. Let your Father remind you of everything He's had for you from the beginning. Give yourself twice the time that you allowed this person to distract you to heal. If he was in your life 6 months, give yourself a year. If he was in your life for 2 years, give yourself 3 years, check your progress, and honestly assess whether you need another year. Accept the fact that it will take increasingly more time for you to get your soul back in order the longer you allowed this thing to rule over you. You've taken accountability. You've actively set yourself up to succeed by denying him/them entry into your life. And you are pursuing God's vision for you. YOU ARE ON YOUR WAY QUEEN! You are God's precious daughter; royalty and a royal priesthood. Never doubt it. And never allow anyone else to cause you to question that ever again.

To move forward sis, you need to make some GOALS. Here's another hard truth: A goal without corresponding action on your part, is just a wish!

If you truly wish to take your life back and allow God to heal you (and yes, whether you were actively taken advantage of, had questionable motives or witnessed any/all of these situations within your congregation, you need to examine yourself closely to determine if your heart needs healing).

To determine if healing is needed, answer the following questions:

1. When I say the word "man", list the mental picture and immediate thoughts that come to mind. Be honest.

____

____

____

____

_______________________________________.

A. Were your thoughts negative? YES   NO
B. Was your mental picture negative? YES   NO

2. What was your last positive experience with the body of Christ?

____

____

____

____

____

_________________________.

A. Was there leadership involved in this experience? YES   NO
B. Do you believe that the experience would have been the same with one of the leaders at your church? YES   NO

3. Who do you seek for wise counsel within the body of Christ?

____

____

____

____

____

_________________________.

A. Did you list one of the leaders where you
    serve?   YES   NO
B. Did anyone where you serve come to mind
    that is not a family member or a friend?
    YES   NO

Review your answers to determine if healing is
needed. For example, the first question is pretty
obvious in its goal to ascertain whether you harbor
resentment against male authority figures in the body
of Christ.

Ephesians 4:31 advises us to let all bitterness,
wrath, anger, slandor and clamor (fussing) be put
away from you along with all forms of malice.
Anger, wrath, slander and fussing are all a product of
a bitter heart. Bitterness is a cancer that eats up a
person from the inside, changes their perception
about everything (good becomes evil and evil
becomes good) and pretty much pollutes the
atmosphere – so much so that – other people are
infected. So, it's worse than just cancerous, it's a killer
virus that only God can save you from.

If you regard bitterness in your heart, take it
immediately to the King and lay it before Him. He is
the only one immune to it. He is the only one that
can help you fix it.

Back to goals.

How about we set goals for how you plan to move forward healed and whole?

There are several kinds of goals, I am only going to cover the three that apply to this section.

Those three are smart goals, product goals and process goals.

Smart is an acronym for: Specific, Measurable, Achievable, Relevant, Time-sensitive. These are the attributes that make sure your goals are accountability driven.

Product goals are your overall smart goal - what it is that you wish to achieve with that goal. What is the product, as in, what will you PRODUCE to show that you've reached your goal?

And then there are process goals. Process goals are three or four mini goals that you plan to observe during the process of striving for your PRODUCT goal. If the PRODUCT goal is the destination, your PROCESS goals are the steps and the map that will get you there.

Make sense? Good. Let's start with your first SMART PRODUCT GOAL: I PLAN TO PUT ACTION STEPS ________________________________ into practice by (date) __________________.

I will do this by (process goals should be listed after the example below).

1. (example: I will set a recurring reminder on my phone to record my voice journal daily by 5 pm Friday, October 5th, 2021.)

____

____

____

____

2. __________________________________

____

____

____

3. __________________________________

____

____

____

If you have had a chance to pick up your Quick-Hit Hard-Truth study guide, turn to the section titled: ALABASTER BOX and continue the exercises there.

Don't forget to find an accountability partner! God wants the best for you, but that starts with YOU!

Section 2: My Powerful Brothers & Fathers

Lesson One: Sisters and Daughters

Michael Shields was single. A single minister. A commodity in his local church that was highly sought after.

Which was a problem. Because as far as Mike was concerned, he didn't ever have to marry. He didn't need to. Women threw themselves at him coming from all directions, walks of life, cultures, and religious beliefs.

In all honesty, the constant talk about his marital status among his family and friends was really starting to get on his nerves.

Why should he be pressured into marriage because of a woman's biological clock?

Paul was an apostle and he wasn't married, right? You didn't see any of the other apostles giving him a hard time about it.

As far as Mike was concerned, he could go forever without having to get married, and would be totally cool in a life with just him and God.

Only one thing stood in his way. He liked women. Women of all shapes, sizes and colors. If he allowed himself, he could look at women for hours.

He loved their smell, the way they sounded... and, he absolutely loved to watch them walk. Coming and going, God knew what He was doing when He'd made woman.

Beyond finding them attractive and, to be honest, good for sex and maybe for cooking (though, he could go to his mom's for that, not to mention; he could hold his own in the kitchen), he didn't see much of a benefit to having a wife.

And yeah, so; his parents got divorced when he was a kid. He had the best of both worlds and was well taken care of. His parents were friends, which had been a blessing, he had to admit. He had three sisters who he loved dearly and, for as long as he could remember, God had been talking to him.

Ministry was an obvious step for him. His family thought so and naturally, so did he. He just wasn't sure where a wife would even fit into the plans that God had for him.

And if it wasn't for the consuming attraction for them, he wouldn't bother wondering.

He didn't hate women or anything. Mike loved women. Too much. More than he wanted to anyway.

If he 'd gone to counselling as his father suggested, he may have discovered why he lived in such a compartmentalized fashion. But he didn't, because he knew what the counselor would say.

They'd say the same thing the counselor his parents had gotten for him during the divorce would say.

All of his issues most likely stem from her. Tonya.

Which just couldn't be true. But that's what Dr. Alvin Swingler told his parents when he was twelve.

It was something that he'd talked to his Pastor, his boys, and even his dad about. They all felt like it was no big deal. And Mike agreed.

So what, she took his virginity when he was ten years old. From where he came from, that was a blessing not a curse.

Except... sometimes, he could see her in his dreams. Biracial and curvy, smelling like something he'd never smelt before. It had been so pretty. She had been pretty. And he had never even looked at a girl like they were anything other than... well, a girl, until Tanya.

Mike had been in Atlanta visiting his cousin Joe, his best friend before his aunt and uncle had relocated.

While he'd always had trouble making new friends, Joe had been the exact opposite. And by the time Mike had gotten to Atlanta for a visit, he could tell the difference between them was apparent.

Joe had two bikes. And that was all he and Mike had needed. If they didn't go everywhere there was to go in Atlanta before Mike came home from that summer visit, they definitely covered enough miles to get Mike at least halfway home to St. Louis.

It was on one of their biking excursions that he'd met Daedae . DaeDae Butler was the youngest hustler he and Joe had ever met. He'd steal candy from the corner store and sell it to the kids in his hood. He'd never gotten caught as far as Mike knew.

Since stealing was wrong, Mike wasn't fond of hanging out with DaeDae.

It had been on a Sunday night, when his aunt had gone to bed early that Joe had urged Mike to ride over to DaeDae's because he had something to show them.

Mike didn't want to go. But the thought of his cousin riding out there alone in the dark wouldn't leave him alone. So, he'd agreed to go with Joe, just to have his back.

DaeDae had been waiting by his back door and snuck them into the basement to watch some movies his older brother had let him have in exchange for a loan.

The titles of the movies made Mike uncomfortable but hey, he was with his boys so, it couldn't be all that bad.

And it hadn't been... bad, per se. At least, not to Joey and DaeDae who laughed and joked the whole time. Apparently, pornography had been nothing new to them.

It was shockingly new to Mike though. He was uncomfortable yeah, but not enough to be made fun of for the rest of his visit in Atlanta. And there was no way he was riding back through the hood alone this late at night.

Feelings he'd never felt in his life assaulted Mike. He played it off of course, laughing and joking with the guys like it was no big thing. But his head felt like it was on fire. His whole body was, in fact.

The boys joked about who would be going to the bathroom first. Mike laughed but he had no idea what they had been talking about.

He found himself crossing and uncrossing his legs. And having to look away from the video to control his breathing.

Which was why he'd almost lost his mind when DaeDae's brother's friend, Tanya, all of a sudden jumped down the steps to scare them. She almost gave him a heart attack!

The two friends that were used to this kind of thing fell out laughing, rolling around on the floor; while Mike had jumped to his feet to race toward the nearest exit.

And that was how he caught Tanya's attention.

All of Tanya's attention.

Looking him up and down, in a baby voice she laughed asking, "Aw, did I scawe da widdle baby? Come give Tee Tee Tanya a hug, its okay baby boy, I gotchu."

She'd hugged Mike's head to her chest so tightly, breathing became a memory. But her hug wasn't like his mom's or his sister's hugs. Nor any of his aunts or the ladies in his church.

This hug made him feel stranger than the movie did. And it wasn't until Tanya dragged him back into the laundry room telling him, "Don't pay those fools no mind, let me make it up to you for scaring you so bad," that he would find out.

All of his friends and even Joe told him that what happened wasn't a big deal. In fact, Joe had been jealous, and so had DaeDae.

And maybe it wasn't. But it had fundamentally changed Mike from that day forward. He saw women now... as women, not just people. It was something that he couldn't unsee. Even his sisters, once he arrived home, looked different to him.

But hey, he was a kid. Stuff happened, you deal, you move on.

Mike wasn't stupid though. His counselor had felt differently and, upon finding out when they were divorcing, his mom had cried... literally cried!

"That such and such abused my baby!" She screamed at his father after he was told to go to his room when she burst into tears.

Mike could hear his father saying, "Lucille, boys are different. Stuff like this happens all the time. It's no big deal. Hush now, you scaring the boy!"

"Oh, so had it been Donetta, Jade or Shonda? What if it had been them somebody put they foul hands on when they were ten? Would you say that then?"

"You know better woman! Anybody touch my daughters they would be wearing six feet a dirt as a lifetime reward! They are my DAUGHTERS Lucille, girls are different. Now stop all this madness before the boy seriously thinks somethin' wrong with him. "

They had gone on and on until finally, his father got so frustrated that he slammed out the house.

Mike had heard his mother cry herself to sleep that night. He'd felt helpless. He couldn't change the past. He should have just kept his mouth shut. All he could do was be the best person he could be going forward. Maybe then his mother wouldn't see him as broken. Maybe she would stop treating him like he had some kind of terminal illness (something that ticked his father and sisters off to no end). And maybe... maybe he could have a normal life without all the drama women seemed to cause others.

Until then... he could look... and try very very hard not to touch. And if he messed up on occasion, God would forgive him. His sins were bought and paid for on the cross. Mike would just do what he always did when he slipped, ask forgiveness and keep it pushing.

***

Okay, my brothers. And fathers. While this is a fictional account; it is a compilation of several stories and accountings from brothers that have had candid discussions with me regarding their first sexual experience. As a group, we sisters wanted to understand.

Our brothers would share, then repeat, as if by rote, "it's no big deal," or "that kind of stuff happens all the time, men are different than women."

Um. No. While that is true, it's not true in the way you think. In fact, a woman's brain doesn't fully develop until she is twenty-five… and men mature SLOWER than women.

Just because a body is ABLE does not mean that the activity is acceptable OR that a boy/man is mature enough to handle the consequences that come with sex.

According to a Kinsey State, College of California study, the average male loses his virginity at 16.9 years of age.

To be honest, for black males (especially urban black males) I firmly believe these numbers are WAY off.

Just in my small world of St. Louis the ratio of males that I have met and, in group discussions surmised, SEVERAL lost their virginities between the ages of ten and four-teen, the majority between ten and twelve.

As a man, there are certain truths that are just accepted. One of which, is that things that happen to men don't impact them; well, impact them much less than they impact women.

That too, is a falsehood.

The consequences of premarital sex carry great weight. In fact, to be clear, the word of God indicates that sexual immorality is the ONLY sin that a man is to RUN from. For everything else, God says, "stand and see the salvation of the Lord,"

But when it comes to sexual immorality? That's not the case. Paul even taught that it is the only sin where you sin against YOUR OWN BODY, thus reaping the consequence of it physically.

Wonder why there are so many sexually transmitted diseases? There's your answer.

Here's the truth – your early experiences with women and girls strongly impact how you perceive women.

I remember, as a teenager I was watching a promo for the comedian Tommy Davidson, where a group of pre-teens were jumping rope in one of the shots.

My brother, sitting next to me glanced up and said, "Ooh, Freaks!"

It took more than four seconds for me to respond (trust me ya'll that is saying something because my tongue could be quick and wicked back then, praise God for the fruit of the Spirit). When I could speak, I immediately disdained with, "those are little girls!"

His response, "Oh, well, little freaks then."

I literally turned red with rage. I had to bite my tongue because my mother was in the next room. It wasn't until years later that I had to wonder, what is it in some men that when they see girls they think "daughter" and want to protect them, versus the man that thinks "freaks", and wants to exploit them?

The answer was a simple one. Experiences and influences shape the way men see girls and women.

Michael's experience produced several situations that created building blocks within his perception where women were concerned.

You could probably tell that Michael's perceptions are based on a black and white model; either something is this or its that. Stealing is wrong. Period. The why doesn't matter. People were people at first. After his abuse at Tanya's hands (and yes, I am calling it what it is; he was abused just as a ten-year-old girl would have been in his stead. And I'm that mama that would have cried and went after Tanya all the way in Atlanta when I found out, don't judge me); as I was saying before you rudely interrupted me (grin) after Michael's abuse, he no longer saw any woman in a particular role. His sisters could no longer be just "sisters". He also saw them as "women"; which is normal for a ten-year-old boy who hasn't developed the maturity to categorize and group individuals.

A therapist once told me that, when a person is sexually or emotionally abused, their growth and emotional maturity are stunted.

Imagine that this is what many of our brothers and fathers have gone through. Add to that, their slower maturity rate in comparison to women.

The end result of such a state is to men that may have experienced this, women are treated like mothers, many of them disdain or dislike women and view them as something to be used for physical release and that is all (as that is their foundational experience), or, they love women... too much.

There are various reactions to situations similar to what Mike went through, however the end result is the same, rarely do they see women as sisters, as treasures, as valuable and something that they should protect at all costs.

Enter the church. With a misogynistic history that actually sanctioned treating women as chattel. Is it any wonder that women are not seen as sisters or daughters to be protected?

Even the Talmud, Jewish ceremonial law and legends allows for child brides to be wed under certain conditions.

And because man said it is okay, we assume that God is okay with it.

Let's be clear. God is NOT okay with his daughter's being treated any kind of way. If He were, why would he have created woman to be man's help meet SUITABLE for him? The word for HELP in the Greek is "paracletos"; very close to the same word used for the Holy Spirit, "paraclete".

Would God be okay with us treating the Holy Spirit in such a fashion? No.

Paracletos basically means to strengthen, support and uphold; kind of like a support beam in the building. If there are any contractors reading this, they will tell you that the support beam is the strongest and yet, the most vulnerable part of a structure.

It keeps everything intact; yet it can be torn down like any other beam. And if it is, the building comes crashing down with it.

Hence God saying, "a man that finds a wife finds a good thing and obtains favor from the Lord."

Women were supposed to be your partners in ministry as well as in the home; to subdue and have dominion; two walking together so if one falls, the other is there to catch and hold them up.

While man is the visionary, women are equipped to catch attacks coming from the north, south, east and west. She processes AS she communicates while men, having a more linear thinking style, need time to process and consider all factors before making a choice. She is the ENEMY of Satan, so she can feel him coming, while YOU are not. You have a powerful being, Man 2.0, given to you by God to help fulfill your mission in the earth! She's such a bad-mamma-jamma, that her only weakness... is YOU.

Don't believe me? Genesis 3 states...

> **13** And the Lord God said to the woman, What is this you have done? And the woman said, The serpent beguiled (cheated, outwitted, and deceived) me, and I ate.

14 And the Lord God said to the serpent, Because you have done this, you are cursed above all [domestic] animals and above every [wild] living thing of the field; upon your belly you shall go, and you shall eat dust [and what it contains] all the days of your life.

15 And I will put enmity between you and the woman, and between your offspring and her [a]Offspring; He will bruise *and* tread your head underfoot, and you will lie in wait *and* bruise His heel.

16 To the woman He said, I will greatly multiply your grief *and* your suffering in pregnancy *and* the pangs of childbearing; with spasms of distress you will bring forth children. Yet your desire *and* craving will be for your husband, and he will rule over you. **AMPC** - *Amplified*

I know, men and women have focused on the "he shall rule over you" part.

But God wants you to look closer. To rule over his home was just as much of a punishment for the man as it was for the woman. No longer were they operating as a team.

Now there would have to be distinctive roles filled by men and women in the home due to Adam's inactivity and Eve's gullibility as Satan engineered "the fall".

The woman was not the only person present when the serpent convinced her to partake. Adam was there also, right next to his wife. Silent (thus complicit). Earlier in Genesis chapter 3 we find this fact made clear:

Genesis 3...

> **4** And the serpent said unto the woman, Ye shall not surely die:
>
> **5** For God doth know that in the day ye eat thereof, then your eyes shall be opened, and ye shall be as gods, knowing good and evil.
>
> **6** And when the woman saw that the tree was good for food, and that it was pleasant to the eyes, and a tree to be desired to make one wise, she took of

the fruit thereof, and did eat, and gave also unto her husband with her; and he did eat. **KJV** – *King James Version*

Adam was right there. With her. Silent when he should have spoken up. Do the words, "Happy wife, Happy life?" ring a bell?

Of course, there is nothing wrong with wanting to make your wife happy; but to the point where you are not operating in your God-mandated (not given, MANDATED) authority? That's not a good thing. That is a garden thing; a thing that God introduced a consequential commandment for man not to do it again.

The balance of that teaching however, is "Husbands, love your wife as Christ loved the Church, willing to lay down your life for her."

Meaning just because God commanded you to rule (which really means that YOU are the one He holds accountable by the way) it didn't mean that you have the right to abuse (broken down – ABnormally USE) his daughters.

Let's get back to the power hidden in your sisters, mothers, and wives.

I have never laughed so hard when a brother of mine joked how I can fill a pantry with twenty dollars.

Women can be amazing economists. They had to be to feed a family of ten off of meager wages back in the day.

As your wife and partner, a woman who understands WHAT she is becomes a dynamic asset, one that your life would be sorely unfulfilling without.

In fact, because we are created to be "Helps" many of us without husbands just help... whoever!

I have brothers that I have helped, causes, ministries, coworkers, sisters... the list goes on and on. Just because we have no husband to help, doesn't mean that those of us that are single DON'T answer the call within us.

I've gone around the block a bit so let me get back to my points.

Some men have a very difficult time seeing sisters in the body of Christ as "sisters".

Looking at the history, I don't really blame them.

But we have to start accepting accountability of this at some point and begin to shift the thinking, retraining our sons to see women for what God created them as, not for what you have been raised to think they are because it's convenient.

If she isn't your wife, my brother, she is your SISTER. And older brothers, these young women aren't "young tender's" in your local church, they are YOUR DAUGHTERS.

Whether you are single or married, this is so; you must begin to hold yourselves accountable in God's house.

God sees and knows your heart; just as He takes note of his broken daughters that come to church, exposed (hoping for validation from you); He sees you looking. Lusting. Something Jesus condemned to be the same as committing adultery.

So, brothers, fathers... what do we do? Is it your fault that some women come to church "to catch," and put themselves out there?"

Not at all. What is? Your looking, lusting, or taking advantage of them.

God will not allow you to use the biological imperative that causes you to think of sex every 4.3 seconds as an excuse.

That is why He gave you His Spirit. One of the fruit that came with the gift of His Spirit is SELF CONTROL (or temperance some versions say).

Am I saying that I am perfect and have always maintained self-control? Nope, not even close.

But like Paul I share the claim that, while I am not saying I have attained this, I press toward the mark of the high call in Christ Jesus, My Lord.

Your sisters and daughters in the church are there for you to PROTECT, not to manipulate or take advantage of. Even those that throw themselves at you.

You are not responsible for their actions, they are. But you ARE responsible for YOURS.

I say this in all seriousness because reasonings and justifications that many have used in the past have caused their hearts to grow hard, callused, and uncaring where God's daughters are concerned.

When that happens, pride enters the picture. And here's another hard truth for you, pride doesn't just go before a fall... Let me pull it from YOUR bible again so you understand the seriousness of pride...

Proverbs 16:18...

> ***Pride goeth*** *before destruction, and an haughty spirit before a fall.* ***KJV****- King James Version*

A haughty spirit or "arrogance" is what goes before the fall, not pride. Nope. Pride goes before DESTRUCTION. I don't know about you, but I can get up from a fall. What I can't do is "un-destroy" myself.

I said all of that to say, if there is a secret disdain or faulty perception of women that you harbor, my brothers and fathers, I urge you, in the precious name of our Lord, to acknowledge it, get rid of it, and be accountable to your Father in Heaven.

Did you know that to CONFESS doesn't mean to provide a list of your transgressions, but merely to agree? Agree with God that you were wrong. Agree with God that your perception of his daughters is skewed and that you've allowed it to stay that way.

Once you do this, you open yourself up to God helping you gain freedom in this area.

The enemy will fight you. He doesn't want you to see the woman as an ally. That is why in the world system, all day long, you'll see some type of battle of the sexes going on.

When men and women join forces, DOMINION happens! To subdue and have dominion means to BRING under control through your God-given authority and to KEEP under your control and reign via your God given authority.

THAT was always God's purpose for Man and his wife.

Trust me when I say, if you work to make women your ally versus your enemy, if you see them as God sees them, as valuable vessels for His glory, a type and shadow of his Holy Spirit, a strong weapon full of *Dunamis* power in His arsenal... your life will change. For the better. I promise you.

Lesson Two: Gateway to Hades

Proverbs 7:21-22

21

*With her many persuasions she caused him
to yield;
With her flattering lips she seduced him.*
22

*Suddenly he went after her, as an ox goes
to the slaughter [not knowing the outcome],
Or as one in stocks going to the correction
[to be given] to a fool...* **AMPC**- *Amplified
Classic*

I almost don't blame the early churches for
their misogynistic views. So far, we have been taught
since we were small children that the woman was
responsible for original sin, and then there are verses
like the one above.

Obviously, the woman is in league with Satan to lead mankind to hades. Right? I mean, who wouldn't think that.

As with so much of God's word and so many of His teachings, much is taken out of context.

Listed here in this scripture of Proverbs is A WOMAN, not ALL WOMEN. Not eve MOST WOMEN.

The scripture, in its entirety discusses how a fool is easily misled by foreign, immoral women. These women do not have the benefit of being raised "in the admonition of the Lord."

They don't know the principles of God's word or who they are.

Even then, if you just glanced up three verses you would read, "Say to [skillful and godly] wisdom, "You are my sister," And regard
understanding *and* intelligent insight as your intimate friends..." **AMPC**- *Amplified Classic..*

Wisdom is to be treated as a SISTER... hmmm. Why do you think Solomon would say to regard wisdom as a sister? What did he mean by that? Maybe that it is something to be cherished? Held close? Protected?

Who profits, truly, from men considering women to be abhorrent, weak, whiny creatures that don't benefit mankind unless of course in the realm of procreation?

Who chances losing DOMINION over the earth if man were to truly recognize in his marriage partner, his sisters, his mothers the phenomenal power housed in them to sense the enemy at work, expose his plots, spiritually protect her home and nurture her visionary by taking on everything else that comes at them while he focuses on the vision?

The answer seems pretty obvious to me.

Yes, there are women that don't know who they are, right there in the front pews even. Giving their married Pastor the eye while being sly around his wife.

Yet there are also men of God who have their wives sharing pews with their mistresses right there in the front pew.

Neither of these scenarios please God. And BOTH carry a consequence. As men and women of God we have GOT to stop seeing each other as competition or the enemy and start working proactively and protectively regarding each other.

Let the world system have their battle of the sexes.

We serve and abide in a whole other kingdom. The Kingdom of God. God's way of doing things.

to move forward in a much better condition (where ascertaining my value was concerned) than when I'd entered our marriage.

The enemy has targeted our women (by this I mean black women especially) with a negative viewpoint widely communicated via media, as well as our own people.

People that do not witness our grace. Our struggle. Our strength. Our fears. Our triumphs.

Many young men, in particular, have adopted the mindset that our women are not worthy of their attention; that dating outside of our race is the only option for them.

I do not condemn dating multiculturally. I condemn anyone grouping ANY person into a negative construct created for the sole purpose of demonizing our race and negatively affecting our ability to reproduce in the earth.

The black woman has only recently regained her pride in her appearance and begun to seize the right to wear her hair how she wants and still be considered intelligent, professional and wise.

It blows my mind how many brothers are willing to leave her, the black woman, hanging with trying to prove her worth to the world, many agreeing with the world at large.

Nevertheless, all women are God's daughters. All of God's daughters have value.

And all men should be protecting and covering them; especially in the body of Christ.

I adjure you, men of God; if you belong to a house of worship where the women are grossly being misused by someone in authority.

As a loving brother and father, confront it; and if it doesn't change, LEAVE IT.

My one last scripture reference for you in this section is Malachi 2:

> "Now, O priests, this commandment is for you. ² If you do not listen, and if you do not take it to heart to honor My name," says the LORD of hosts, "then I will send the curse upon you and I will curse your blessings [on the people]. Indeed, I have cursed them already, because you are not taking it to heart. ³ Behold, I am going to rebuke your seed, and I will spread the refuse on your faces, the refuse from the festival offerings; and you will be taken away with it [in disgrace]. ...
>
> ⁷ For the lips of the priest should guard and preserve knowledge [of My law], and the people should seek instruction from

his mouth; for he is the messenger of the LORD of hosts. ⁸ But as for you [priests], you have turned from the way and you have caused many to stumble by your instruction [in the law]. You have violated the covenant of Levi," says the LORD of hosts. ⁹ "So I have also made you despised and abased before all the people, just as you are not keeping My ways but are showing partiality [to people] in [your administration of] the law."

God does not change. He is the same yesterday, today, and FOREVER. Not only are those abusing their authority cursed, THEIR PRAYER over YOU is cursed!

Dear brothers and fathers, I would not wish this on any one of you.

To be silent is to be complicit, as Paul was at the stoning of Christians by holding people's robes.

Silence in the face of authority misusing their positions to take advantage of God's people carries its own weight and consequence.

For Paul, it was loss of vision and, regaining that, a life full of tribulation standing for what he formerly condemned.

God wants better for you. Do not ignore his call to accountability.

Determine in your hearts to confront the evil in love. If your words were not received and there is no indication that change will occur, shake the dust off your feet as a testimony against that place, take your family and LEAVE.

God is bringing judgment to his house first. The flagrant abuse of authority will not stand. Do NOT be a part of those experiencing the wrath of God.

I will close this section with ACTION STEPS, things you can do to put yourself onto this road of accountability. As always, this may not be your struggle; it may be someone you know however, that needs to hear this. Gift them this book. Be their accountability partner. Whatever you do, don't fail them by not speaking out in love. To be caught up in the eye of God's judgment is a terrible, terrible thing. Please do these things before it is too late.

To all my brothers and fathers that already serve as protectors, thank you. Thank you for protecting me when I was new to the faith and didn't know my own value. Thank you for seeing the talent hidden away within me like a diamond in a piece of coal. Thank you for patiently mining it with me, so that I could discover what God wanted me to become.

I say this for all of my sisters and mothers that may not have had the opportunity to share it. While I have shared it with my spiritual and physical father and brothers, I don't think that this gratitude can be expressed "too much."

We need you. We act tough; and the women's liberation movement wants to feminize you, but don't doubt for a moment that, we; the women that know better, NEED you.

Without you, there is no us. You are MAN 1.0. There could never have been a 2.0 otherwise. We may have apps and run on 5 g speed, but we are vulnerable, breakable... we need the hard case of your protection, durability... DEPENDABILITY; while we spend our lives doing what we do... making you look GOOD (Proverbs 31).

So, don't let the enemy win. Hold yourself and all our brothers and fathers accountable. By doing this, you honor God, you honor yourself, and you show us love.

ACTION STEPS:

IF you have found yourself in these situations:

6. **SEEK WISE COUNSEL** – find someone that you know will keep your confidence and partner with you in being accountable for your choices, to pray with you, and to help support you as you consider what God is saying and how He is directing you to confront the issue within yourself, your congregation, and the body of Christ.

7. **SEEK GOD** – He loves you. He will never leave you nor forsake you. Willingly give to Him all the issues of your heart. He binds up the broken hearted and heals all their wounds and sorrows. He knows what you need, and He will be there to help you break the chains, habits, lusts, and painful attachments that you secretly harbor (ex: pornography addiction).

8. **CUT TIES** – Let it go. I'm talking about your past. The women that hurt you. The women that spoke negatively about you. The women that belittled you or disrespected you. Forgive. Bitterness, anger, anxiety... every negative emotion you can think of stems from holding

grudges. Let them go. Block out the voice of the ENEMY and begin to study God's word on the subject. Listen to great teachers teach on it. Strengthen your faith and speak words of life over yourself. You have the power, no matter what anyone tells you. And if your house of worship is a source of many of these negative emotions? Ask God if He wants you to leave or stick in and deal. Whatever the answer, I promise he will be with you the whole way. And when God is with you, He is more than the world against you.

9. **STAY FOCUSED ON GOD** – pursuing a relationship with a woman when you have issues stemming from your childhood is a tricky thing. Seek counselling and keep your focus on God. Don't wrap yourself entirely in someone else. Learn who YOU are in Christ. Use your smart phone as a recording journal. Voice record your daily progress. How you feel, what God is saying, scriptures you read, and what your accountability partner has counselled you to do. Play all of them again every four weeks. You will hear your voice growing stronger, more confident, less riddled

with confusion and, instead, filled with the renewal of God's presence. Mark the dates on your calendar that you notice a change. You're starting to see women differently. You're able to go places without feeling a sense of rejection. Mark every victory as the Lord emotionally heals you. I promise you won't regret it. You deserve better, and this is the perfect time to focus on you. Focus on you allowing God to show you what BETTER looks like.

10. **USE YOUR TOOLS** - Last, use the notepad in your phone (or buy a journal) and start writing. Write down what your dreams and desires were before you were distracted or detoured. Write down goals you'd lost sight of along the way and how God is now redirecting your desires back to it. Remember single brothers, you're not seeking another relationship right now, you are seeking healing, wholeness, and restoration. Let your Father remind you of everything He's had for you from the beginning. Give yourself twice the time to heal. Do not rule out therapy as a tool if you need it. There is no shame in that.

Accept the fact that it will take time for you to
get your soul in order. You've taken
accountability. You've actively set yourself up
to succeed by denying the enemy his plan
regarding your life and where you serve. And
you are pursuing God's vision for you.
YOU ARE ON YOUR WAY KING! You are
God's powerful SON; royalty and a royal
priesthood. Walk it out. I dare you. I double
dare you! In Jesus' Name!!!

To move forward brothers and fathers, you need to make some GOALS. Here's another hard truth: A goal without corresponding action on your part, is just a wish!

If you truly wish to take your life back and allow the mind of Christ to develop where your sisters and daughters are concerned, you need to examine your heart and mind closely to determine where an error in your perception lies.

To determine if you need to change your perception, answer the following questions:

4. When I say the word "woman," list the mental picture and immediate thoughts that come to mind. Be honest.

____

____

____

____

_______________________________________.

C. Were your thoughts negative? YES   NO
D. Was your mental picture negative? YES   NO

5. What was your last positive experience with the body of Christ?

____

____

____

____

____

_____________________________.

C. Was there female leadership involved in this experience? YES   NO

D. Do you believe that the experience would have been the same with one of the leaders if they had been female? YES   NO

6. Who do you seek for wise counsel within the body of Christ?

____

____

____

____

____

_____________________________.

C. Did you list one of the leaders where you
    serve?   YES   NO
D. Did anyone where you serve come to mind
    that is not a family member or a friend?
    YES   NO

Review your answers to determine if further action is needed. For example, the first question is pretty obvious in its goal to ascertain whether you harbor resentment against women or women in authority in the body of Christ.

Ephesians 4:31 advises us to *let all bitterness, wrath, anger, slandor and clamor (fussing) be put away from you along with all forms of malice.* Anger, wrath, slander and fussing are all a product of a bitter heart. Bitterness is a cancer that eats up a person from the inside, changes their perception about everything (good becomes evil and evil becomes good) and pretty much pollutes the atmosphere – so much so that – other people are infected. So, it's worse than just cancerous, it's a killer virus that only God can save you from.

If you regard bitterness in your heart, take it immediately to the King and lay it before Him. He is the only one immune to it. He is the only one that can help you fix it.

Back to goals.

How about we set goals for how you plan to move forward in the right mind regarding your sisters and daughters?

There are several kinds of goals. I am only going to cover the three that apply to this section.

Those three are smart goals, product goals and process goals.

Smart is an acronym for: Specific, Measurable, Achievable, Relevant, Time-sensitive. These are the attributes that make sure your goals are accountability driven.

Product goals are your overall smart goals - what it is that you wish to achieve with that goal. What is the product, as in, what will you PRODUCE to show that you've reached your goal?

And then there are process goals. Process goals are three or four mini goals that you plan to observe during the process of striving for your PRODUCT goal. If the PRODUCT goal is the destination, your PROCESS goals are the steps and the map that will get you there.

Make sense? Good. Let's start with your first **SMART PRODUCT GOAL: I PLAN TO PUT ACTION STEPS** _________________________________ **into practice by (date)** _________________.

I will do this by (process goals should be listed below the example).

4. (example: I will set a recurring reminder on my phone to record my voice journal daily by 5 pm Friday, October 5th, 2021.)

____

____

____

____

5. _____________________________________

____

____

____

6. _____________________________________

____

____

____

If you have had a chance to pick up your Quick-Hit Hard-Truth study guide, turn to the section titled: BROTHERS AND FATHERS and continue the exercises there.

Don't forget to find an accountability partner! God wants the best for you, but that starts with YOU!

Section 3: Servants of the Most High God

A Prophetic Warning and Encouragement From the King of Glory:

Apostles, Prophets and Pastors... Ministers, Evangelists and Teachers...

Beloveds, you are the heart of God's heart. And His love for you is infinite.

But His patience is not.

Hear my heart as I relay this message. And remember that I speak from the valley and not the mountaintop.

God is not pleased. He is not pleased with the rampant disobedience in His house. Not just in the congregation, but those He has hand selected, chosen to lead.

He has chosen us to lead, teach, comfort, encourage, empower, war for, and strengthen His people.

We had one job. To mature the babes in Christ into Kingdom ambassadors: Kings and Priests, knowledgeable in operating with wisdom, integrity and power as Jesus did.

He gave us the gauntlet, and centuries later sees our digression in the way.

Regurgitated milk and mashed up food from God's word is NOT healthful for the body.

Yet, instead of the house of God being filled with powerful kingdom ambassadors, it is full of individuals whose growth have been stunted.

God's people experience malnutrition, regress in understanding, and learn over and over the doctrines of their BIRTH and BAPTISM into Christ versus learning their responsibilities as citizens in the Kingdom of God.

WE are sorely in error. WE have found it easier to control children. Because even an heir is under the care of servants until they come of age to rule and reign.

As children, they remain powerless. Unprotected. Unable to fulfill the mission that God sent them into the world to complete.

Because as leaders, we have found them easier to control that way.

I repeat for emphasis so that you can hear me: GOD IS NOT PLEASED.

Paul experienced the frustration that we, as leaders should be experiencing. The people should have been eating the meat of God's word; yet they were still in need of the milk. Relearning, again and again, the doctrine of salvation, forgiveness and baptisms.

We ought to be incensed that God's people have been stuck in the third grade of His Kingdom way of doing things for CENTURIES.

Our messages and sermons have become how-to books full of catchphrases and nuggets of truth. Milky truth.

Our people are stuck at the cross where their story BEGAN, not ended.

those of us that have been lazy as the bad manager parable indicated; those of us that have been deceived and have become deceivers to God's people.

Our days are numbered. Judgement begins at God's house.

To assume that He is God, thus the judgment would be manageable is a horrible assumption. Do not mistakenly assume His grace nullifies the power and consternation of His judgement.

For our God is the same yesterday, today and forever. He is not merely the God of the earth or our Universe. He is the ETERNAL GOD and King.

Thus, his warning. WE ARE BECOMING THE CHURCH OF LAODICEA in Revelations.

If we do not change our direction and soon, judgement will fall from our King and will not stop until He has fulfilled the time ordained for it.

No number of cries for mercy will change it. Leaders will fall away or expire, a great falling away will be the result of this judgment.

This is not a warning that God is pronouncing just through me. Several of those that serve within the prophetic are receiving the same message.

God promised that He would not do anything in the earth without telling His prophets.

Hear me. He is telling us. And if you are prophetic, you should be hearing the same urgency of this call.

I am commissioned by our Father as a scribe to send you, those He loves, this message.

TURN IT AROUND NOW! Step down if you must; give leadership over to those operating in integrity. It is better to lose eyes, hands, limbs, than to lose Christ.

WE are fortunate that we have been given an opportunity and a small window to address our error before these events occur.

Remember, once judgement starts, it cannot be waylaid, cannot be avoided and it cannot be stopped.

Even as I write this, I do it with much grief at the end result of this call. As this truth is directed at ME as well as all of God's leaders.

I feel the sharpness of the sword, the word of God, as a double-edged sword, it cuts both coming and going.

DO NOT ignore this warning. The shift is coming. The great falling away is coming. The entire structure of "church that we know it" is changing as Covid-19 has clearly proven.

We will not be returning to business as usual.

God is taking His people in a new direction, and we must be prepared to move with the cloud and the fire from within; His guiding Spirit; in unity.

Please hear me. Our King does not lie. He does not fail. Share this message and, if you have not, begin to live a fasted and prayerful life.

As with any great shift, fasting and prayer are a necessity to ensure that we are following God's plans. It is our duty to prepare for this new season.

The harvest has always been ripe. It is the laborers that Christ adjured are few. We must be prepared, as laborers, to catch those falling when leaders begin to fall from grace or expire due to their continued disobedience.

We must be prepared to snatch those disillusioned from the fire. They will be lost, and we need to be prepared, as under shepherds, to go out and find them.

A message to those that have purposefully set up immoral and evil systems within your houses of worship. Abusers of men, women, CHILDREN...

God is not only NOT pleased; your judgment is sealed. You have purposefully and willfully disobeyed God and caused harm to befall HIS people. Because you have had NO regard for Him, not only are you cursed, but your prayers (though sincere) over those that serve in your house of worship are also cursed.

The people do not flourish because of your actions. The land will grow desolate and God will wipe the name and legacy of your ministry out of the memories of man as a witness and testimony against you. This is what God says. And His word will not return to Him unfulfilled.

A message to those in leadership having immoral affairs; God is not pleased.

Why have you allowed yourself to be so deceived? Why have you allowed the enemy to pollute the purpose, the original intent, of your calling in the Lord?

Your Father urges you to come home. Remove the root of evil in your life, reject the lies that have created the strongholds you seek comfort in when those that He has sent to you confront you.

Each day your heart grows colder, and your thoughts scatter as your light dims. Give Him back what is HIS. YOU are His. You are His son, His daughter, His child. Come back home. Repent, remove the evil, and reject the hold of the enemies lies while you have the opportunity now to do so.

I say this with tears in my eyes. I know how compelling people that you feel you love can be.

But she is not yours. He is not yours. They belong to the Lord, as do you. And because you are rejecting the wife of your youth, the husband of your youth; God does not hear or regard your prayers.

Everything you put your hand to will sour. Any victories you have will be short lived and produce the exact opposite of what you expect.

Because you are His child who has lost sight of your purpose. He wants to restore you. Let Him. Again, this is a matter of urgency. There are choices that cannot be unmade. Don't allow your inactivity to become a choice that can never be reversed.

***

Thank goodness, that part is done. I hate that family. Pronouncement of God's judgment is a weight that carries a heavy sense of grief with it. It is almost as if you feel the consequences as God communicates them. Moreover, I feel HIS grief. I can feel our Father's heart breaking behind his steel resolve.

I praise Him that He is my comfort as we got through the previous section.

Now, a message of hope. A shift is coming beloveds, not to our evil, but for our good and protection.

We have clearly read the signs of the times and can confidently assess where we stand in history.

Now is our time. We are ambassadors but we are also Kings and Priests. We operate in the Kingdom of the most high God. It is now time for us to become kingdom economists that operate in wisdom and self-discipline.

It is time for the babies to GROW UP. To become active entrepreneurs, suppliers and distribution centers for Gods people. WE are to become MEDIA REVIVALISTS, KINGDOM BUSINESS ENTREPRENEURS and a NETWORK of Kingdom supply and demand.

Hear His call. You are the HEAD and NOT the TAIL. It is time for you to mature into the HEAD, our true head, Christ Jesus.

It is time that Christ has a body that can bear the weight of His authority and His mission.

Trials will come. It is inevitable that the dark increase in order for the light to become that much more apparent.

Hear the Father? He is calling you into a place of preparation. More time with Him, less on social media, television, games or time wasters. He is demanding more of you. He is calling us into position.

I urge you family, to fast and spend as much time in prayer EVERY DAY that you can with the Father. He has an impartation for you. A specific mission to declare to you. And His undying love to convey to you. Hear Him. Seek Him. Draw near to Him.

Seek Him while He may be found. I promise you, He will meet you half way. Just start. And start today.

God loves you. I love you. We must be available as a resource to one another during this time, be as one, just as Jesus prayed.

God bless you and keep you. I pray with you that we are all prepared for the times that are to come. I pray that your heart is healed if you also, have been hurt by a leader, and I pray, In the name of Jesus, that you grow in full power into the purpose and plan that Father has for you as we move into this new time.

Thank you for reading and thank you for hearing what our Father has to say. I will see you soon family, if not in this life, then in the next.

Amen.

Author's note:

Hello Family!
This quick-hit, hard truth book was written during a thirty day fast for our people, our nation and God's vision for us.

It is during this time that much of what was communicated in section 3 was provided by our Father.

This book being the first in the quick hit, hard truth series, I did not take the composition of it lightly.

Normally, I compose faith-based fiction, adverts for which you will see at the end of this book.

But I had a mandate to fulfill. And I answered the call.

Now I'm trusting you to share this word and answer the call that the Lord our God enlists you to fulfill.

I pray this in Jesus' Mighty Name. Amen

C. M. James is a pseudonym for Chantay M. Hadley, also known as author, Chantay M. James and C. Marie Evans.

Winner of the Praize writing contest in 2005, she published her very first novel and has been writing ever since. A jack of many trades - all centering around educating and assisting children - she has also served in many areas of ministry. Combining her passions of serving Christ and writing, Chantay strives to help others and to be an influence to those that can use encouragement to become all that they were intended to be.

A devoted mother of one, she lives in St. Louis, Missouri, coached Middle School Basketball and loves a good romance, a good laugh... and cartoons.

Don't forget to sign up for the Midwest Creations Publishing Quarterly Newsletter on our website!
www. midwest-creations-publishing.square.site

MWCP UPCOMING RELEASES AND AUTHOR LIST:

Adair Rowan
(Sci-Fi, Suspense, Science and Tech)

- Concentric Relations: Unknown Ties – March, 2019

Projects for Adair:

- Project Ariel

Chantay M. James
(Romance, Sci-Fi and Suspense)

Available to pick up your copy today:

- Valley of Decisions
- Waivering Minds, Book 1: Brainwaiver Series
- Waivering Lies, Book II: Brainwaiver Series

- Brainwaiver Beginnings shorts: Wattpad (Chantay M. James)

Projects for Chantay:

- Waiverings, Brainwaiver Series (Anthology includes novella 1.5 and 2.5).
- Waivering Eyes, Book III: Brainwaiver Series (December, 2020)

M. Renae
(Christian Living, Marriage, Divorce and Family)

- Allowed 2 Cheat: When Marriage Takes A Wrong Turn.
- Allowed 2 Cheat: Study Guide
- Allowed 2 Cheat: Workbook

C. Marie Evans (Black Romance and Action)

- A Hater's Prayer (July 2019)

C. M. James (Nonfiction/Christian Living)

- Who Broke My Daughter's Alabaster Box?

Projects for **C. Marie Evans**:

- Annie B.'s Legacy (December 2020)
- Legally Bound (July 2021)
- C.J. Series – Action (2020/2021)
    - CJ Run
    - CJ Hide
    - CJ Fall
    - CJ Rise

Projects for **C. M. James**:

- He Still Breaks Chains: Quick-Hit Hard Truth Series, Book 2 (December 2020)
- Cracked Pot Communication for Fractured Folks: Quick-Hit Hard Truth Series, Book 3 (April, 2021)
- The Power of No: Quick-Hit Hard Truth Series, Book 4

<u>Pastor Melba Boyd</u>
(Christian Living, Counselling)

- The Root of Pain – November, 2020

<u>Teresa Taylor-Williams</u>
(Christian Living, Devotionals)

- Praize in a Pandemic: Overcoming Covid-19 (Devotional), December, 2021.

And many more authors are coming soon! Don't forget to check out the website for author swag, events and giveaways!

Stay tuned for bits and pieces of some of our publications!

Author Chantay M. James and the Brainwaiver Universe!

What if you could have anything you desire? Is what you desire worth everything you possess – including your soul?

Waivering Minds, Book I:
Brainwaiver Series

Celine:

A Licensed Clinical Social Worker in Alton, Illinois, Celine Baltimore lives a content, peaceful life. Until one of her patients reveals that her sister has become a guinea pig for behavior modification technology known as "Brainwaiver," then disappears.

Left with a child's journal that paints her once comfortable life in horror and intrigue, Celine finds herself nose deep in corporate secrets, shifty attorneys and rugged, intense men (specifically Enoch Sampson or Sam for short).

Shocked that she's named a winner in the Brainwaiver contest (a contest she'd never entered) Celine learns of more missing children in Alton and their link to the hip new software trying to take over her life; including Sam's teenaged son.

An all-around goof that can't stop tripping over her Aubusson rug (or keep said rug straight) can Celine let go of playing it safe, fight the good fight of faith and get the guy in the end?

Sam:

A widower and ex-CIA agent turned owner of a family owned construction company, Sam picked up a few skills from his former life. Some he wishes he'd never learned. Espionage and secrets had been his business.

Missions and sacrifice had become his life. Growing cold again seemed inevitable… until he met goofy (and determined) Celine Baltimore.

Could he avoid that place of unfeeling and do the unthinkable? Retrieve his son and love again? Because protecting his family was the only thing that mattered to Sam.

It was something that he would do at any cost. It was more than a goal – it was a promise. And Sampson men ALWAYS kept their promises.

Waivering Lies, Book II: Brainwaiver Series

Max:

Max Arpaio is a Freelance Information Systems Security Analyst and part time Bounty Hunter on occasion. When Max responded to Enoch Sampson's call for help to find his missing son he realized something crucial.

The top government secrets and plots he'd stumbled upon long ago are no longer a shadow on the horizon.

And Now that Denise Ferry has taken up the gauntlet to wage a silent war against Brainwaiver, Max has to make a choice: To help the woman he loves but can never have or stand aside and watch as millions are led like sheep to a slaughter. Either way, he's a dead man. It's only a question of when.

Balboa:
Denise Ferry is a Business Consultant, former FBI agent and a severe pain in Max's rear. A woman who has gone from gang member lieutenant to military strategist to agent, she could write a book on espionage and silent war strategies.

So, when Denise engaged in a search and retrieve mission that targeted children for mind control experimentation, she's in for the long haul to wage war. However, she hadn't counted on warring on two fronts: Against the advances of Brainwaiver and to win the heart of Max Arpaio.

A man of mystery with a sense of doom, Max draws Denise despite her efforts to fight the attraction. Can she help him overcome his dark past?
As a strategist she realizes she has no choice. Without him taking her back against Brainwaiver, she's already lost the war before she starts. And without him in her life she's already lost her heart.

Valley of Decisions: A Valley Series Novel
by Chantay M. James

St. Louis, Missouri. Home of the missing.

Sandra Peters, editor for Re-born magazine, has planned her life to the smallest degree - her work, her friend, and her faith.

But when the prominent Christian magazine goes belly up and her friend attempts suicide, Sandra watches all of her plans crumble.

All she has left is her faith and her calling. For some reason, God has chosen her, a woman with an abusive past, to journey to St. Louis to save children. But how? And from what?

These questions plague the jaded young editor as she treks to find her destiny.

Little does she know that her war is not with flesh and blood. Little does she know that only self-sacrifice, unity, and love can defeat the evil that consumes the next generation.

Little does she know that, in the heart of St. Louis, lies her Valley of Decisions.

Concentric Relations: Unknown Ties

Psychotherapist Dr. Liam Ronaw enjoys a rather plush existence until new client's recite details about night terrors and dreams. Several dream descriptions spark a memory from his childhood. In an effort to help these clients, he follows the various clues as he works to figure out what connection they have to his own past.

Dr. Ronaw follows the breadcrumbs which lead him into a world involving a global coverup, a hidden community and a terrible new threat, the likes of which could spell doom for all life on earth.

Welcome to The Hater's Prayer Saga by author C. Marie Evans!

The Hater's Prayer

Naomi Carmichael Nee' Brooks was a Hater.

Well, a reformed hater, that is.
Destiny, her sister had been deemed by her church, family and all creation "the golden child," so Naomi knows how it feels intimately and repeatedly to have someone steal her thunder.

And now that she was about to be a divorced mother of three, struggling to make it on a state job, with an ex that was all about rubbing her nose in it, Naomi wouldn't know what to do if God hadn't given her what her and her bestie called, "the hater's prayer".

With a podcast that's growing by the hundreds, Naomi is sure that life was on the upturn. But she should have known better.

Falsely accused of hurting her kids, her ex-husband coming after everything she's got (which isn't much) and her (not really) hated sister sexually assaulted at a club; all while Victavious "Vic" Carter, the boy next door, has suddenly decided she's the one, can Naomi fully let go of her hater ways, trust God instead of herself, and give her old friend a chance to "shoot his shot?"

As a reformed hater, all by herself she doesn't have a chance. But with her bestie at her back and crazy family at her side, Naomi knows one thing to be true: With God, all things are possible. And seeing Vic through new and enlightened eyes, that may just include falling in love again.

Don't sleep on Allowed 2 Cheat: When Marriage Takes A Wrong Turn by Author M. Renae!

Allowed 2 Cheat: When Marriage Takes a Wrong Turn

I loved my husband. Looking back, maybe I loved him a little too much. Definitely more than I loved myself. How do I know? Because six weeks before our wedding I found out that there was another woman.

Devastated, I called him crying, trying to understand why. He explained that she started off as a friend because I made him give up his best friend (another woman and as such, a different story entirely, but really the same situation) to comfort me. He goes on to explain that it just turned into more than he expected and how he couldn't stop it since he didn't want to hurt her. He said that he did it to try and get it all (by all I assume "the cheating") out of his system so that he wouldn't cheat once we were married.

I knew then, in my heart, that his cheating would continue for a lifetime. But I was determined to keep the love I thought I found. I was so eager to hold on to that love that I told him, "I forgive you and we will get past this." Sadly, that wasn't the last time I spoke those words.

Throughout the course of our marriage, that refrain was repeated if not openly, silently… over and over again. So, this is my story.

To protect those I love the most, I've changed names (including mine, just because) and the locations of various events. I also did this because the names are not important, neither are the places.

What holds true, or at least the truth that I'm trying to convey is illustrated in the message of this allegory. A message that so many women need to hear. A message outlined in the following fact that, as you read, you will feel this in your very soul:

BECAUSE I was aware of my husband's cheating during our engagement and set no boundaries or consequences; I gave him permission and consent to continue it during our marriage. I didn't walk away, and I should have. As a result, ten years later I'm still struggling with my sanity and choices.

Don't be me.

Allowed 2 Cheat: When Marriage Takes a Wrong Turn – Study Guide

This is the study guide to be read in accompaniment with the novel adapted memoir Allowed 2 Cheat, When Marriage Takes A Wrong Turn by M. Renae. (Memoir by M. Renae; Novel written and adapted from the memoir by Chantay M. Hadley and Midwest Creations Publishing).

Allowed 2 Cheat: When Marriage Takes a Wrong Turn – Workbook

This is a companion workbook for Allowed 2 Cheat: When Marriage Takes A Wrong Turn (the memoir adapted novel as well as the study guide).

Learn key skills that will assist you on your journey to healing from damaging relationships.

With fun exercises and a journaling component built in, your quality time with God will take on a whole new meaning!

Freedom, joy and emotional stability can be yours! Don't forget to pick up the novel and the study guide for a richer and more fulfilling experience.

Coming Soon:

Waiverings:
A Brainwaiver Anthology

Celine Baltimore and Sam (Enoch) Samson introduced the world to the Brainwaiver Universe in Waivering Minds, a place full of mysteries involving missing children, mysterious technology and race against time to save one from the other, never realizing that the target, in truth was Celine. And as mysteries often do, the saga didn't end with Celine and Sam...

Waivering Winds, Book 1.5:

Waivering Winds sheds light on the in-between-times, connecting Waivering Minds to book two of the Brainwaiver Series, Waivering Lies.

Delilah and KC's story.

As Celine's opposition, Delilah did her thing in Waivering Minds, but it wasn't all good... and surprisingly, it wasn't all bad either.

Learn about her horror story compiled of kidnapping, human trafficking and present day slavery. God and KC have their work cut out for them when it comes to winning Delilah's heart.

But neither one of them is about to give up. Read her story as God and KC show a woman hurting from the pain of her past that she is more than who she thought she was...

Waivering Times, Book 2.5

Novella 2.5 begins midway through Waivering Lies, Book two of the series.

Amanda and Cruz's Story.

Amanda, too young and too focused on saving the world from Brainwaiver (starting with her mom) finds Cruz irritating... and irresistible.

On a mission from God, Amanda is determined to win her war, and the man that makes her wish she never had to fight one.

However, Cruz Arpaio is no fool. Amanda, at nineteen, was too young for a US Marshall in his mid-twenties.

Not to mention that Denise "Balboa" Ferry-Arpaio, his new and military trained sister-in-law would kill him, if his brother Max didn't first.

So, Cruz left as he was told.

Years later, he still can't get the thought of Amanda Same out of his mind.

Determined to return for the woman he knows is his, Cruz never makes it to his destination.

What happens next turns the worlds of Amanda Same and Cruz Arpaio on its head; and kicks off the war that had been a long time coming.

Will Cruz and Amanda find each other again and somehow, reunite and reignite the powerful attraction that both of them can't forget in these Waivering Times?

Only God knows...

www.ingramcontent.com/pod-product-compliance
Lightning Source LLC
Chambersburg PA
CBHW052041150726
48002CB00002B/701